UPON THIS ROCK

Dr. Scottie E. Jackson

ISBN-13: 978-1492213949
ISBN-10: 1492213942

TABLE OF CONTENTS

ACKNOWLEDGEMENTS

I am grateful to the following people who assisted me in this work:

My wife, Darlene Jackson, who typed and edited my manuscript meticulously, while offering much-needed advice and encouragement here and there.

My daughter, Sharon Jackson, who proofread this paper and gave great, refining suggestions.

GLOSSARY

Altar of Incense. The Golden Incense Altar was made of acacia wood overlaid with gold. It was situated just in front of the Vail, the curtain which separated the Holy Place from the Holy of Holies, inside the Jewish Temple. It was the place where the priests were required to burn incense in the morning and at twilight, as a perpetual fragrance before the Lord.

Ark of the Covenant. Described in the Bible as a sacred container wherein were placed the Tablets of Stone containing the Ten Commandments, Aaron's rod and manna. It was seen by the Jews as being the presence of God among His people.

Freetown. It is the capital and largest city of Sierra Leone in West Africa. It was founded by Lieutenant John Clarkson and freed American slaves who were brought by the Sierra Leone Company in 1792.

Kisumu. It is the third largest city in Kenya in East Africa. It is located on the eastern side of Lake Victoria.

Lord's Prayer, The. Properly the Disciple's Prayer that Jesus taught to His disciples. It is a model prayer for Christians today.

Matatu. It is a mini-bus or other public transportation in the nation of Kenya. The word in Kiswahili means "taxi."

Mount Nebo. The name of the mountain from which Moses beheld the Promised Land.

Rock of Gibraltar. Sometimes called the Pillar of Hercules or by its Latin name Calpe. It is a monolithic limestone promontory located in Gibraltar, off the southwestern tip of Europe on the Liberian Peninsula.

Wailing Wall. The remains of the great Jewish temple in Jerusalem, Israel where many go to pray. Sometimes called the Western Wall, it is the most holy place for the Jews today.

INTRODUCTION

Today we are going through great problems in our country and throughout the world. Everything is unstable from the economy to issues of morality. The future looks bleak for many who have lost homes and jobs. The news has been filled with reports of people living in "tent communities" because of the loss of their homes. Others that have lost jobs cannot find other jobs due to the closing of so many businesses. However, in spite of all these situations we face, God is still the One who is in control. If we will trust Him and have faith in Jesus as Savior, the Lord will make a way for us where there seems to be no way. The bottom line is—He is our Rock.

Jesus said, "Whosoever cometh to me, and heareth my sayings, and doeth them, I will shew you to whom he is like: He is like a man which built an house, and digged deep, and laid the foundation on a rock: and when the flood arose, the stream beat vehemently upon that house, and could not shake it: for it was founded upon a rock." (Luke 6:47-48 KJV) Those that put their trust in Jesus and live according to the Word of God, build their lives upon a rock and that rock is Jesus. In this ever-changing world, there is only one who never changes; He is the Rock—Jesus Christ.

This Rock has many facets. The four we will address here are essential to who we are in Christ—The Rock of Revelation, The Rock of Testimony, the Rock of Prayer, and the Rock of Faith. The specific passages on which these are based are taken from Matthew and are in chronological order except for the Rock of Revelation. I begin with this one because I feel that it was and is of utmost importance for followers of Christ to have the revelation of who He is. This is the greatest foundation stone of all because without Jesus being the Son of God there would be no rock at all.

In His temptation, Jesus was tested by the devil in the wilderness and through that testing became a testimony that stands sure even for us today—our Rock of Testimony. When Jesus taught His disciples about prayer, He gave them a foundation of how to reach the heart of the Father and to know Him, not just know about Him. This is our Rock of Prayer. After we know Him, it only stands to reason that a part of our foundational experience is our faith in Him. We soon realize God does not just want to work for us, but through us and with us. He invites us to be a part of what He is doing in the world today as He is our Rock of Faith.

Chapter 1

The Rock of Revelation

In Matthew Chapter Sixteen Jesus asked his disciples "Whom do men say that I, the Son of Man, am?" And they said, some say that thou art John the Baptist: some, Elias; and others, Jeremias, or one of the prophets." (Matthew 16:13 KJV) John the Baptist was such a great figure that many, including Herod Antipas, believed he might have come back from the dead.[1] Some said Jesus was Elijah. Jews to this day believe Elijah will return just before the Messiah comes.[2] The feeling was just as strong then. However, Jesus was not the forerunner spoken of in Malachi Chapter Four, He was the Messiah Himself; the answer for which mankind was looking.

Others said they thought Jesus was Jeremiah. Before the exile, Jeremiah had taken the Ark of the Covenant and the Altar of

---

1. William Barclay, "Vol. 1," in *The Gospel of Matthew*, The Daily Study Bible Series (Revised Edition; reprint, Philadelphia, PA: The Westminster Press, 1975), 136.

2. Ibid.

Incense and hidden them in a cave on Mount Nebo. The Jews believed that at the coming of the Messiah, Jeremiah would return and bring them back and that the glory of God would return to the people again.[3]

This is similar to the way church people are today. They want things to return to the way they used to be, but what God wanted to do was fulfill His promises to them. How often I hear someone say, "We had such a great revival years ago. I wish it would happen again." The truth is that God wants to do something greater, more magnificent than we have ever seen before. We should not settle for yesterday's manna. We need a fresh touch from Him each and every day.

Many Christians these days are way too busy working for God, but not spending time with God. In order to know Him and see a move of God, we must develop that intimate relationship with Him by praying, praising, fasting, and having time alone with Him in the Word. Preaching one more sermon, visiting one more nursing home, going on one more mission trip will not be as

---

3. Ibid.

effective if we have not taken time with the Master. When you spend time with Him, then you will be prepared and filled with the anointing to get the job done.

Others of Jesus' day thought He was just another prophet. Sometimes even today, there are folks who are looking for another prophet with another "word" from God that will give them the answer they need or want. However, Jesus is not just another word or way, He said, "I am the way, the truth and the life; no one comes to the Father except by me." (John 14:6) He was the manifestation of God and has all the answers that we will need in this life. When we know Him, He will answer our prayers, meet our needs, and reveal to us His plan for our lives.

After Jesus had listened to what everyone else was saying about who He was, "He saith unto them, But whom say ye that I am?" (Matthew 16:15 KJV) His disciples had heard everyone else's opinions, now was the time for them to decide for themselves. Jesus put them on the spot.

We often are swayed by the thoughts and opinions of the people around us. If they go to church frequently, we go with them. If they make excuses and stay home, we stay home as well.

If they read the Bible and do devotions each day, we will implement that as well, but if we do not get around to doing it, it is not a big issue for us. This is because it is not done as unto the Lord, but in competition and comparison of ourselves with others. Jesus wants followers who are not moved by trends or public opinion, but will be led by Him.

Simon Peter was the only one that spoke up to give an answer to the question Jesus asked. The others obviously sat there dumbfounded. How sad it is that they had been with Jesus all of this time and did not have a full revelation of Who He was. However, many are like that today. They have been going to church for years, have joined a local church, and are even paying tithes, but do not really know who Jesus is.

I was such a person. I was brought up in church, was taken to Sunday school and church every Sunday without fail. My father was a church trustee and deacon. My mother was a Sunday school teacher and the church treasurer. I was baptized and joined the church when I was twelve years old. In our church, if you went to the altar it was assumed you would join the church and take membership. No one counseled me to see if I had made a decision for Christ.

When I was seventeen years old and a junior in high school, I participated in a production of "Camelot". It was a big success. In fact we were asked to do repeat performances. About two weeks after the play was over, the director decided to host a cast party at the local American Legion. It was a night of dancing, snacking and party fellowship. While at the party I noticed a group of people off to the side sitting in a circle. I thought I would go and check out what was going on. Maybe they were sharing some juicy gossip or telling the latest off-color jokes. I wanted to find out, so I pulled up a chair and became a part of the group. I waited to hear what scandalous talk would reach my ears.

To my great surprise they were not talking about anything dirty or evil, but they were speaking about Jesus. They said they felt out of place at the party and did not care who thought they were "Jesus freaks." Some were even telling about what God had done in their lives. This made me uncomfortable and I wanted to quickly get up and leave, but I could not move from my chair.

That night after I got home and got in bed, I could not sleep. I tossed and turned all night under the conviction of the Holy Spirit. At about 5 a. m. in the morning I heard the voice of the enemy say, "If you will just ignore this, it will go away." After a day or two the conviction was gone, but God was not finished.

A few months later in August, our church was having Vacation Bible School. The meetings were held in the evenings. The teenage group that I was in had their classroom time first and it just happened to be led by the same lady who was our teen Sunday School teacher. Before the class began, we were all having a wonderful time talking. Most of the kids in the class were life-long friends. We had grown up in church together and also attended school together. As the teacher opened the class, she stood up and addressed the class, "How many of you know for sure that you are saved?" We were all taken off-guard. I think only two students stood up and I was not one of them. I had never been put on the spot like this about my salvation. I was a church member, had been baptized, and came to church faithfully. No one had ever questioned my relationship with the Lord, although I had

had my own doubts. Now everyone knew I had not stood up. What would they think? Who would they tell?

After the class was over and we went to the fellowship hall for refreshments, I went over to my teacher and said, "I don't know that I am saved. Would you please be praying for me?" She said she would. The next day after my parents had gone to work, I bowed beside the couch in the living room and gave my life to Jesus. The weight of sin lifted from my shoulders and I knew I had a relationship with Him.

How wonderful it is to know the Lord! Once you have entered into relationship with Him, there comes a peace and joy that no one can take away. Once we know it, we must begin to speak it. Peter said, "Thou art the Christ, the Son of the living God." (Matthew 16:16 KJV) Up until this time maybe Peter had just assumed Jesus was just a great teacher or the latest prophet, but now by divine revelation he knew that Jesus was the Christ: the Anointed One and Messiah promised to Israel. He was God's own Son come to earth.

Now Peter did not just say that He was the Son of God, but that He was the Son of the living God. Here the word *living* is from the Greek work *dzaho* which means *to live or be lively*.[4] He is a God that is active, energetic, full of life and movement. Praise the Lord, we serve Him who is full of power and is continually moving in the lives of His people. This living God stepped out of heaven and into the earthly realm in the person of Jesus.

The Jesus answered Peter, "Blessed art thou Simon Bar-Jona for flesh and blood has not revealed this unto thee, but my Father which is in heaven." (Matthew 16:17 KJV) Simon Peter received the knowledge of who Jesus is by revelation, man did not tell him. It is interesting that when Jesus speaks to him in this text that He calls him "Simon Bar-Jona" or Simon, Son of Jonah. It is almost as if He is saying, "Your father did not tell you this, but my Father did." So often we acquire knowledge from parents, teachers, preachers and other acquaintances. Most of it is very useful, but tends to be biased from the point of view of the one who is sharing. Revelation knowledge is not tainted by the opinions of others, but comes directly from God.

---

4. James Strong, "Greek Dictionary of The New Testament," in *Strong's Exhaustive Concordance of The Bible* (McLean, VA: MacDonald Publishing Company, n.d.), p. 34, #2198.

Jesus then said to Peter, "Thou art Peter, and upon this rock I will build my church…" (Matthew 16:18 KJV) I personally like how the Amplified Bible says it, "I tell you, you are Peter [Greek, *Patros* – a large piece of rock], and on this rock [Greek, *petra* – a huge rock like Gibraltar] I will build My church …" (Matthew 16:18 AMP) On revelatory faith like Peter's, the Church would be built. Without it the Church would not be constructed on a firm foundation and would crumble and fall.

In the same way, churches today that are not built on the solid Rock will not last. Sometimes we are amazed by a church in our area that has quick growth. This can be good if it has been solid growth, but if the crowd was drawn by gimmicks and built on sensationalism, it will not survive the storms of life or the testing of the Holy Spirit. I often tell pastors that slow growth can be the best kind. When a church is at the beginning stage, the Lord will bring in foundational members who will catch the pastor's vision and be of like precious faith. If the church is not firm in its foundation, it is a church that will have many problems and most likely fail.

The Church should not just be a local social club. It should be a collection of those who have heard the voice of Jesus Christ and now have a very personal relationship with Him. The word *church* in Greek is *ekklesia* which means *a calling out.*[5] If we have been called, we should no longer be a part of the world system – acting, speaking and thinking like the world. We should be different and set apart—blazing with holiness unto the Lord.

In the Gospel of John, Jesus said to Nicodemas, "Ye must be born again." (John 3:7 KJV) The word *again* in this verse is *another*. It means *from above* and has the implication of *from the first.*[6] All too often Christians get saved and even join a local church, but keep on living the same life they lived before. If you have been born again, you have been born from above and now belong to a Heavenly Kingdom. Do not waste time trying to fix up the old life; recognize that He has made all things new. It is like you had never lived before you knew the Lord. Paul said in his second letter to the Corinthians, "Therefore, if any man be in

---

5. Ibid, p. 26, # 1577.

6. Ibid, p. 13, # 509.

Christ, he is a new creature: old things have passed away; behold, all things are become new." (2 Corinthians 5:17 KJV) What a wonderful revelation to know the old is gone and buried, and we have a brand new life ahead!

In the last part of Matthew 16:18 Jesus declared about the Church, "The gates of hell shall not prevail against it." (Matthew 16:18 KJV) There are two very interesting facts I have found about the gates of a city. First, the gates of the city in ancient times were the strongest part of the city.[7] This tells us that the strongest part of hell cannot succeed against the Church. I have many times heard people stand and testify in church, but their testimony was all the bad things the devil has been doing in their lives. These were not good testimonies for they only give glory to the works of Satan.

Even when the enemy has caused damage in our lives, we need to recognize we serve a powerful God who will give us victory in every situation. If your child is on drugs, start praising

---

7. John McClintock, and James Strong, "Vol. III - E, F, G," in *Cyclopediea of Biblical, Theological, and Eccesiastical Literature* (New York: Harper & Brothers Publishers, 1883), 51.

God that He will be delivered, saved, and called into Christian service. If you have just lost your job, begin to thank God for your next job that will have better pay, greater benefits and will be located closer to home. If you are sick, begin to declare that by His stripes you are healed according to 1 Peter 2:24. Some say this verse is only talking about spiritual healing (salvation), but it is also talking about our physical healing. The word *healing* in Greek is *iaomai* which means *to cure or make whole*.[8] Jesus has come to make us whole in body, soul, and spirit.

After you have believed the Word, you must begin to declare it. Rev. Lloyd Ashby of Sanford, North Carolina tells of a man he knew from a church in Fayetteville, North Carolina who had a hideous tumor growing on his face. He was prayed for by a visiting evangelist and, although there was no noticeable difference, he began to praise God and testify in every service that he was healed.

Months passed and there was still no change, but he kept claiming he was healed and praising the Lord for what He had

---

8. Strong, *Strong's Exhaustive Concordance of The Bible*, p. 37, #2390.

done. Finally, one night he stood to testify once more. Many in the congregation were probably thinking, "Here he goes again." Little did they know this night would be different. While he was testifying of his healing, the tumor slid off of his face and his face was left as smooth as a new born baby's. Praise the Lord! He had believed what God had said and confessed it. If we stand on the foundation of the Word of God, we will never be ashamed and all of the tactics of the enemy will not succeed against the Saints of God.

The second interesting fact about the gates of the city is: in ancient times of the Eastern World, the gate of the city was the place where the elders and rulers of the city gathered to give counsel and justice would be served, similar to a modern-day court room. Often the punishment would take place right there.[9] Many decisions are made everyday in hell against the people of God. However, we have Jesus' promise that those plans will not prevail against the Church. As we believe God's Word, we will see His

9. Barclay, "Vol. 2,"*The Gospel of Matthew*, p. 143.

destiny for our lives unfold and the lies of Satan defeated by the blood of Jesus Christ.

Then Jesus said, "I will give you the keys of the kingdom of heaven…" (Matthew 16:19 KJV) The person who has possession of the keys is the owner and has the authority over the property they unlock. He can lock or unlock the doors at his own discretion. When I was twelve years old, my mother got a public job for the very first time. Up until that time she had always been a homemaker and was at home every afternoon when I arrived from school. Her job required her to work until five o'clock in the afternoon which meant she would not be there when I got home. At this time, my parents presented me with my very first key chain. It had all of the keys that would fit the doors to our home. I now had privileges I had never had before. I could unlock the doors of our house and enter at my own will. I felt extremely grown up coming in by myself, getting my own snack, and watching television until my mother got home. There was only one problem; I kept leaving my keys at home. So when I arrived from school I could not get in by the door. I would need to get the step ladder out of the storage building outside of our home and go around to each window to see if at least one was unlocked so I could climb in through it. Because I did not take keys with me, I forfeited my right to enter in through the door.

Many Church folks are like that today. They do not have their spiritual keys with them, so they are always struggling in their Christian walk. If they would pray, fast, read God's Word and fellowship with other believers that walk in faith, they would be able to take the keys Jesus offers and walk with authority and live in victory. Jesus said, "If you ask anything in my name I will do it." (John 14:14 KJV) Here the word *name* is the Greek word *onama* which means *character or authority.*[10] When we pray and claim His promises after we have been changed by the character of Christ and are operating in His authority, we will see positive results. Also, if we have the character of Christ it will change even what we pray for and about. Often we are asking for material things when we should be asking for souls and for nations. It is good to have a nice house, new car, and a prosperous job, but none of these things will make you happy if your priorities are not right

---

10. Strong, *Strong's Exhaustive Concordance of The Bible*, p. 52, # 3686

with the Lord. Jesus said, "But seek ye first the kingdom of God, and his righteousness; and all these things shall be added unto you. (Matthew 6:33 KJV) If we are looking to do things God's way and seeking to be righteous like Him, God will add all the things we need.

Verse Nineteen in Chapter Sixteen of Matthew goes on to talk about binding and loosing. The word for *bind* here in the original language is *deo* which means *to bind or tie*.[11] When we begin to speak the Word of God and pray over situations that are not right, we are binding them up and preventing them for coming to pass. As a child, if I wanted to do something my friends were doing but my mother did not agree with, she would say, "That won't happen." She was putting an end to any of my plans that were going in the wrong direction. In the same way, we must put an end to anything in our lives here on the earth that is not like the Lord Jesus Christ.

Jesus also said, "And whatsoever thou shalt loose on earth shall be loosed in heaven." (Matthew 16:19 KJV) Just as you tie

---

11. Ibid, p. 21, # 1210.

something up when you bind it, when you loosen it you untie it. Untying something is to give it freedom. The devil has bound up much in the lives of the saints. We can begin to speak to these situations and freedom will come to them. He will untie what has been tied up as we begin to believe and declare the purposes of God. He wants our lives to be lived according to heavenly principles.

Chapter 2

The Rock of Testimony

We are proven to be a disciple of Christ when we go through temptation. Without going through these situations, we are like children who have not been disciplined. A few years ago, I was working out regularly at a local gym. A good friend of mine said he would like to work out with me. He said he wanted to lose weight and build stronger muscles. I had been doing a routine of walking two miles on the treadmill and then doing reps on all of the cardio equipment. After about two days of working out with me, my friend began to complain about how hard it was to walk on the treadmill. He would stop after only one mile. He then would walk over to the other side of the room where guys with huge biceps were lifting enormous amounts of weights. He would stand and watch them for long periods of time as though that would help him get stronger and build muscles. We had only exercised about three more times when he stopped coming. He was not willing to undergo the discipline that was necessary to get what he desired.

Often preachers preach and teach about the great miracles Jesus did. We are quick to share how He healed the sick, cleansed the lepers and raised the dead. We even like the places where He healed and delivered great multitudes. However, we tend to forget that right after he was baptized in the Jordan River and before He began His ministry, He went through a time of great temptation. This time of being tried would prepare Him for the great ministry that lay before Him.

In Matthew 4:1 – 11, we see the temptation of Christ. In Verse One it says, "Then was Jesus led up of the Spirit into the wilderness to be tempted of the devil. (Matthew 4:1 KJV) Immediately after getting baptized and receiving His Father's approval for being our obedient example, Christ went through His foundational testing. We must note here that it was the Spirit that led or guided Him into the wilderness. Many times we go through a wilderness experience in which we are faced with great temptations, and we are quick to place all of the blame on the devil. The truth is that the enemy can do nothing unless he is allowed by God. Even in the example of Job, Satan had to have permission before he touched Job's life. "And the Lord said unto

Satan, Behold, all that he hath is in thy power; only upon himself put not forth thine hand. So Satan went forth from the presence of the Lord." (Job 1:12 KJV) The devil desired to see Job fall, but God had to give His permission.

It is usually while we are going through our wilderness experience that we undergo the greatest temptations. When we have experienced the struggles of this life and are worn out physically and spiritually, the enemy will use this to his advantage and will attack us and have us question our walk with the Lord. The name *devil* is from the Greek word *diabolos* which means slanderer or false accuser.[12] Just as with Job, the devil comes to accuse us before the Father.

Verse two says, "And after He had fasted forty days and forty nights, he was afterward an hungered." (Matthew 4:2 KJV) When Jesus had not eaten for forty days, He was at an extremely susceptible point in His life. There is no record of Satan coming to Him during the forty day period, but only at the end. For most people, things seem worse when you have not had enough food,

---

12. Ibid, p. 22, # 1228.

sleep, or support. Jesus is now alone, hungry, and tired. This is a vulnerable time for Jesus, who could have fallen into temptation and not fulfilled the plan of the Father.

The enemy came with the first temptation. "He said, If thou be the Son of God, command that these stones be made bread." (Matthew 4:3 KJV) Here we see that the first thing the enemy wanted to bring into question is Jesus' position as the Son of God. He will do the same with us. He will say, "If you are really saved, do this or that." In doing this, he hopes to make us doubt God if the situation does not turn out as we expected. He told Jesus to turn the stones into bread. In the desert where Jesus was, there were little pieces of limestone rock that looked just like little loaves of bread.[13] The devil took advantage of this to make Jesus hungry after a long fast. He does the same with us. He tries so hard to make us desire images that are not even the real thing, in order to get us side-tracked from the purposes of God. Jesus was tempted here to use His power selfishly and for His own use.[14] Thank God He did not give in to that temptation, but stood strong.

---

13. Barclay, "Vol. 1," *The Gospel of Matthew*, p. 66.

Many times today we see those who have great talents, money, or fame, use these for their own purposes and greed. I was recently talking with a minister friend about how many country and rock n' roll vocal artists started out singing as children in church. God gave the talent, but they decided to use what God gave for their own gain. In the end, a lot of them have had drug and alcohol addictions, multiple marriages, and some have even taken their own lives.

Jesus had an answer for the devil. He knew the Scripture and was able to recall it in a time of crisis. How good it would be if we could do the same! There are passages in the Word of God that address every problem and situation we will ever encounter. Jesus said, "It is written, Man shall not live by bread alone, but by every word that proceedeth out of the mouth of God." (Matthew 4:4 KJV) In other words, man needs more than just physical food to satisfy him. It will fill up the body, but not the soul. How often we use food and other things to try to fill a void that only God can

---

14. Ibid, p. 67.

satisfy. Spending time in His Word, even committing it to memory, will transform us and prepare us for temptation.

When our Lord did not give into the first temptation, the tempter decided to do something different. He took Jesus to the highest part of the temple in Jerusalem. There he said to Him, "If thou be the Son of God, cast thyself down; for it is written, He shall give His angels charge over thee and in their hands they shall bear thee up, lest at any time thou dash thy foot against a stone." (Matthew 4:6 KJV) Notice that again the enemy called the position of Jesus as the Son of God into question – trying to provoke Him to jump from the pinnacle of the temple. This type of sensational act had happened many times before. Numerous men, declaring they were the Messiah, had tried such melodramatic stunts in order to get attention. Simon Magus had even promised to fly through the air and had died in the attempt.[15] Here Jesus was tempted to use His power in order to get attention for himself and draw all eyes to see His great power. This would have been putting God to a foolish test. The place that the Father

---

15. Ibid, p. 69.

had for Him and His ministry was to bring restoration to the peoples of the earth so that the name of the Lord God Almighty would be lifted up.

Some people, when they find out we belong to a Pentecostal church, want to know if we handle snakes. If I want to joke with them a bit, I will say, "Just on fifth Sundays." Most of the time I just say, "No." Handling snakes and drinking poison as a proof of spirituality is only putting God to a foolish test. If someone tried to poison you or a snake bit you unwittingly, as it did Apostle Paul in Acts 28, the Lord would protect and deliver you.

A long-time minister friend of mine, Viola Weidemann, tells in her book, *Girded with Strength*, how on a mission trip to Nepal in the 1980's, she and her team ate in the house of one of the leaders in a village where they had been preaching. What they did not know was that he was a Hindu witch doctor and had heavily poisoned their meals. He watched them, waiting for one of them to drop dead, but no one even got sick. When someone from the team returned to the village later, the witch doctor admitted what he had done to the missionaries and said, "Those people have more power than I do." A few months later he gave his life to Jesus Christ.[16]

We also see that Satan knew how to quote Scripture. He will come with the Word of God and quote it out of context, trying to persuade us to make an improper or premature move. Living according to the whole counsel of God and listening for His voice will help us make the right decision every time. Jesus knew all the Word of God and answered, "It is written again, Thou shalt not tempt the Lord thy God." (Matthew 4:7 KJV) Because He was familiar with the entire teaching of the Scriptures, He had an answer even when it was quoted out of context and for the wrong reason.

As soon as the second temptation was over, the devil looked, once more, for something with which to entice Jesus. "Again, the devil taketh him up into an exceeding high mountain and sheweth him all the kingdoms of the world, and the glory of them." (Matthew 4:8 KJV) I believe at this time Jesus saw all the vast empires of the world with their wealth, beautiful structures,

---

16. Viola Weidemann, *Girded With Strength* (Hagerstown, MD: McDougal Publishing Company, 1997), 131.

and military strength. The sight of these must have been spectacular and tremendously overwhelming. For forty days He had been in the desert where there was nothing, but then He saw all of the kingdoms of the world. This was a temptation to compromise and give in to the need for power, which must have been great for Jesus at that time. Everything of substance was far away and in His desperate state, everything probably had such a look of splendor.

As those who follow the Lord, we must not give in to the temptation to compromise for money, position, or power. No matter how difficult life may seem at the time, we must remember the call of God. I have known a good number of preachers who were firebrands of holiness, preaching the Word without fear or favor of the man's opinions. Then I have watched as they became popular, gained great wealth, and were standing behind prestigious pulpits. Their message began to change. In order to stay in favor with man, they compromised the message and the truth of God's Word. They became accustomed to the money and prestige while losing sight of the heavenly vision.

In Verse Nine, Satan says to Jesus, "All these will I give thee, if thou wilt fall down and worship me." (Matthew 4:9 KJV) The devil promised Him everything He has seen on the mountain. However, it is just like the enemy to promise you everything and give you nothing. The Bible says in the Gospel of John, "The thief comes only in order to steal, kill and destroy." (John 10:10 AMP) His whole mission is to take, not give. If he offers you anything, there is a tremendous price to be paid for what you receive from his hand. The price for Jesus would have been to fall down and worship Satan. The word for *worship* here in the Greek is *proskuneo* which means *to prostrate oneself in homage.*[17] In order to have gotten anything from Satan, He would have had to bring Himself to a ground level position. All would have been lost, even our salvation.

"Then Jesus said, Get thee behind me Satan: for it is written, Thou shalt worship the Lord thy God, and Him only shalt thou serve." (Matthew 4:10 KJV) The way to deal with the adversary is not to entertain him, but like our Lord, tell him to be

---

17. Strong, *Strong's Exhaustive Concordance of The Bible*, p. 61, # 4352.

gone. James 4:7 says, "Submit yourselves therefore to God, resist the devil, and he will flee from you." (James 4:7 KJV) We first must be subject to God. Trying to come against Satan without the power of the Holy Spirit, which comes from living a life of complete submission to God, is a losing battle. If we have His presence, we will have His power. The Bible says, "Ye are of God little children, and have overcome them: because greater is he that is in you, than he that is in the world." (1 John 4:4 KJV) If God's Spirit is in us we can overcome every work of the enemy, because He is greater than the devil.

Then Jesus said, "Thou shalt worship the Lord thy God, and Him only shalt thou serve." (Matthew 4:10 KJV) We often forget that our primary purpose in life is service to God. We easily get caught up in many activities, some of which are good. If we are not careful, all of our strength, time, and attention have gone into some other service besides service to God. A servant, in Bible times, could only serve the Master – his time, belongings, and many times, even his family did not belong to him. They all belonged to the Master.

After these three great temptations, the enemy left Him. Jesus stood true to the Father's plan for His life and to the written Word of God. This is exactly what God wants for us to do. If each Christian would stay true to the Lord's purpose for his life and stand on the Word of God, victory would be won every time.

This was not the end of Jesus being tempted of the devil. In the Gospel of Luke we are told, "And when the devil had ended all the temptation, he departed from Him for a season." (Luke 4:13 KJV) The enemy was not gone for good, but the testing that would be the foundation of His life and ministry had been accomplished. If we have come through great testing in our Christian walk victoriously, we will possess a solid foundation in our lives.

When the temptations were over and the angels had ministered unto Him, Jesus began His ministry. "And Jesus returned in the power of the Spirit into Galilee: and there went out a fame of him through all the region round about." (Luke 4:14 KJV) Because Jesus had stood firm and overcame, He came back from the wilderness with the power of the Spirit. The word *power* here is from the Greek Word *dunamis* which means *miraculous power.*[18] Out of trial and temptation was born the miracle ministry of Christ Jesus. Let us do likewise--using the tests of this life to step into a daily walk of miracles.

18. Ibid, p. 24, # 1411.

Chapter 3

The Rock of Prayer

Prayer seems to be a lost art among many people, even Christian, these days. We may say grace before our meals and recite our bedtime prayers, but we can lack severely in our personal, intimate communication with God. The Lord longs to know us in a personal way and the path to developing a relationship with Him is through prayer. All great men and women of the Bible and all of the prominent Saints throughout Church history were people of prayer.

Jesus, even though He was the incarnation of God, was also a great man of prayer. Before and after each miracle recorded in Scripture, we often read of Him going apart to commune with the Father. In the Gospel of Matthew we read, "…He went up to a mountain apart to pray: and when evening was come, he was there alone." (Matthew 14:23 KJV) This time of prayer is just after the feeding of the five thousand and before He walked on the water.

These miracles were the result of spending time in prayer. The results that prayer yielded for Jesus will be the same for us.

Jesus was the One who taught His disciples to pray. They asked Him to teach them after they had observed Him praying. “And it came to pass, that as he was praying in a certain place, when he ceased, one of his disciples said unto him, Lord teach us to pray, as John also taught his disciples. (Luke 11:1 KJV) It is interesting to note that they were provoked to know more about prayer after they had watched Him pray. Our example is of utmost importance in challenging others to grow closer to God. It is nearly impossible to impart something spiritual to someone else unless you have experienced it yourself. Jesus was the great example of prayer and had much to give to His disciples.

I, personally, like Matthew’s outline of the Lord’s Prayer, so is the one we will observe here. However, it is also recorded in the Gospel of Luke. It begins, “And when thou prayest, thou shalt not be as the hypocrites are: for they love to pray standing in the synagogues and in the corners of the streets, that they may be seen of men. Verily I say to you, they have their reward.” (Matthew 6:5 KJV) In Bible times in Israel, prayer was of great importance.

The only regret of the rabbis was that it was not possible to pray all day long.[19] Even today we can get caught up with the long prayers and how to pray "the best" prayer.

When I was a young boy, there was a prominent deacon in our church. When he was asked to pray during the service, his prayers were very eloquent. He used adjectives I had never heard before and even used King James English including "thees" and "thous." I can remember thinking, "I will never be able to pray like he does." I was sure that in order to pray properly it would have to be as fancy as that deacon's. As the years passed, I got saved and grew in the Lord, and realized it was not just the words I said that were important, but that they were said from the heart and out of a relationship with the Lord. In this verse Jesus clearly rejected the prayers of hypocrites. The word *hypocrite* here is taken from the Greek word *hupokrites* which means *an actor under an assumed character.*[20] God does not want us to pray as if we are

---

19. Barclay, "Vol. 1," *The Gospel of Matthew*, p. 191.

20. Strong, *Strong's Exhaustive Concordance of The Bible*, p. 74, # 5273.

putting on an act that is well-rehearsed. He wants to hear prayers that come out of dedication and love – prayers from the heart.

Jesus went on to reveal that these same kind of people love to pray in places where they can be seen of others. Indeed, there are church folks that are the same today. They will take part in ministry activities if there will be a big crowd to see them and thus grant them recognition for all they do. Jesus indicated that this is their reward. The word *reward* here is from the Greek word *misthos* which means pay for service.[21] Those who desire acknowledgement for their acts of service have all the pay they will receive, because their need for attention is the central focus of what that they do.

In Verse Six, Jesus changes the focus to how to pray correctly. He said, "But thou, when thou prayest, enter into thy closet, and pray to thy Father which is in secret; and thy Father which seeth in secret shall reward thee openly." (Matthew 6:6 KJV) Jesus suggested going into a closet to pray. I can remember being very confused by this verse when I was a young Christian.

21. Ibid, p. 48, # 3408.

My closet was small and pretty cluttered, not at all a place I could picture myself praying. However, this is quite a different closet spoken of in this Scripture. The word in the Greek for *closet* is *tameion.* It is a chamber of an oriental house on the ground floor or interior. It was used for storage or privacy.[22] We need to go to a place where we can have the most privacy with God when we pray. In that place we can get to know Him in a very intimate way. There we can speak to Him, and He will speak to us. This does not mean that we cannot pray out loud in church or other places as well. It just means that we should not get in a crowd and pray in order to get attention. My great-grandfather, Richard Faro Blackman, was a wonderful, born-again Christian and a deacon in his church. He never prayed in public because of this verse.

Jesus indicated that secret prayer will be rewarded openly by the Father. Many versions of the Bible leave out the word "openly" in this verse. Leaving it out changes the meaning. The word *openly* here is from the Greek word *phaneroo* which means *externally, publicly, or outwardly.*[23] When we pray in secret and

---

22. Ibid, p. 72, #.5009.

touch the heart of God, He will reward us publicly. How often have I seen men and women of God, who had little money and few financial connections, get air tickets for mission trips abroad, nice clothes, or a new vehicle just because they knew how to pray! Others jealously wondered, "How did they get that? Who did they ask?" Hebrews 11:6 (KJV) says, "For he that cometh to God must believe that he is, and that he is a rewarder of them that diligently seek him." The Lord knows our hearts and will reward His people, so everyone will know they belong to Him.

When my wife and I became engaged, we were part of the staff of Calvary Pentecostal Tabernacle in Ashland, Virginia. I had gone there seven years before to be trained in ministry and had not owned a car during that time. Now most guys who are getting married already have a car and the young lady he is to marry usually expects him to have one. I was blessed that God gave me a bride who already understood living by faith and had also given up everything to serve the Lord. One Sunday morning after arriving back to the campground from attending service in Richmond, we

---

23. Ibid, p. 75, # 5318.

were standing in line waiting to be served our lunch when a lady, who did not live at the ministry, came up to us and said, “Have you been praying for a car?” We said, “Yes, we surely have.” We had been praying privately. She went to sit down and have her lunch. We got our lunch and sat down at another table. When we were finished, but still sitting and talking at our table, this same lady came over and sat down with us. She looked at us very seriously and said, “God has spoken to me to give you my car.” We sat there in amazement, almost thinking we had misunderstood what she had said. By that evening, we had the vehicle in our possession. How faithful is the Lord! No one knew we were praying for a car, but He made a public showing of what we had asked of Him!

This passage goes on to say in verse seven, “But when you pray, use not vain repetitions, as the heathen do: for they think that they shall be heard for their much speaking.” (Matthew 6:7 KJV) Many people have the idea that the more one prays and repeats prayers over and over, the more likely it will be that God will hear and answer. The truth is that God hears you the first time you pray. After I have asked God for something, the next time I pray about it, I thank Him for doing what I have asked of Him. When we pray in faith believing, we should know our God will always answer our prayers.

When He answers sometimes He says 'Yes,' sometimes He says 'No,' and sometimes He says 'Wait.' We tend to like it when God gives an immediate 'Yes.' Some Christians can even be heard boasting, "I prayed; and God acted immediately!" It is really nice to get a quick answer. In our prayer meetings here in Colonial Beach, we have been getting tremendous answers to our prayers. Often we pray for needs on Wednesday night at prayer meeting and by Thursday evening I get a call that the prayers have been answered. Here are a few examples: one Wednesday night, Alice Elliott, who is our Church treasurer, requested prayer for her step-father who had just been diagnosed with bladder and prostate cancer. He was devastated and had called her from his home in Ohio asking for our Church to be praying for him. We prayed fervently that night, knowing that the Lord had heard our prayers. On Thursday evening my home telephone rang and it was Alice. She said, "I just received a call from my step-father. He went back to the doctor today for more tests and an evaluation of his case.

When the doctor saw him today he found no sign of cancer!" Praise the Lord! God is faithful!

Another time a lady in our Church on a particular Wednesday night brought a prayer request for a minister in Cedar Bluff, VA. His doctor had found one of the arteries to his heart was totally blocked. Surgery was scheduled for the next morning. Our group prayed the prayer of faith agreeing in Jesus' name for his healing. On Thursday evening I got a call from the lady, who had just gotten a call from a friend in Cedar Bluff who reported that the minister had checked into the hospital early that morning for surgery. Before the doctor began surgery, he decided to check one more time to verify the exact location of the blockage. When he did, the exam found no blockage at all! Being a professional in his field, he was very puzzled and declared adamantly, "I know there was a blockage." We had touched the heart of God who is the Great Physician.

We like it when God says 'Yes', but what about when He says 'No'? Sometimes we ask God for a certain job, a particular house, or even a particular person's hand in marriage. We are sure He will grant our petition. We pray constantly without results. We rebuke and bind the devil. Finally, in frustration, we question our own faith. In many cases like this, the reason we have not received the answer to prayer is because God is saying 'No.' We need to recognize when the Lord is saying 'No,' but usually we have our minds made up in a particular direction and believe God should agree with our determination. However, that job we wanted so badly could keep us from going to church on Sunday. That person we wanted to marry might turn out to lack the same commitment to God that we have. We need to recognize, when God closes a door, it is His perfect will for our lives, and the God we serve wants better for us than we want for ourselves.

When I was a young man, I was in love with the girl next door. I was sure everything pointed in the direction of us becoming man and wife. After I had prayed about it, the relationship seemed to get better, so I thought it must be the will of God. I felt it would surely happen soon, but suddenly everything began to fall apart. She told me she was no longer sure of our relationship and did not want to see me anymore. I tried very hard to reconcile, but she would not hear of it. During that same time, a co-worker invited me to her church. It was a Pentecostal church and the power of God really moved there. The service was strange and different, but I knew that the people there had a sincere relationship with God, so I kept going back to visit. A few months later I went to a camp meeting in Ashland, Virginia where I received the baptism of the Holy Ghost. From that moment the direction of my whole life changed. I accepted the call to preach and began preparation to work for the Lord. That weekend I also met a red-haired, teenage girl selling books and tapes just outside the auditorium. Her name was Darlene Brabrand and, almost nine years later, she became my wife. She was God's plan for me, and what a blessing it has been to work in the Vineyard of the Lord together! The girl I had wanted to marry those many years ago has been married and divorced twice and is not serving God. What a blessed man I am that God said 'No.'

Finally, sometimes the Lord says 'Wait.' Many Christians, including myself, would rather have God say 'No' than 'Wait.' We need to learn patience on this journey with Jesus. When I first went into the ministry, nearly twenty-eight year ago, many powerful men and women of God prophesied of what Jesus would do in my life and ministry. Many of those things did not happen soon after they were spoken, but today many of those words from the Lord have been fulfilled and I am walking in the promises of God.

Those that know Jesus should not pray like those that are unfamiliar with the Lord. We must be those who are in fellowship with Him continually and intimately. Some folks pray as though they are giving a “Wish List” to God. They list all their wants to the Father every time they pray. It is so good to know the He already knows what our needs are before we pray. But, He does want us to ask because we are His children. Jesus said, “And whatsoever ye shall ask in my name, that will I do, that the Father may be glorified in the Son. (John 14:13 KJV) We should not use His name to “name and claim” things. The word for *name* in this Scripture is the Greek word *onoma* which means *character or authority.*[24] When we begin to ask of God, we need to do it in the character and authority of Christ. We need to ask ourselves, “Would this request be after the character of Christ or after my fleshly desire?” I feel we often ask for “toys” when we should be

---

24. Ibid, p. 52, # 3686.

asking for souls. When we ask in His authority, it must also be with His character. When we do not receive what we ask, most likely it is because we are asking out of a selfish desire. James Chapter Four Verse Three says, "[Or] you do ask [God for them] and yet fail to receive, because you ask with wrong purpose and evil, selfish motives. Your intention is [when you get what you desire] to spend it in sensual pleasures." (James 4:3 AMP) Oh, if our desires were God's desires, how many and powerful would be the answers to our prayers!

When I was growing up, our pastor would open every Sunday morning service with prayer and at the end of that prayer he would say, "And as you taught us to pray…" and would then lead the congregation in The Lord's Prayer. We will now examine that prayer from the Gospel of Matthew. The Lord's Prayer is not a child's prayer. It also is not the Family Prayer. The Lord's Prayer is specifically and definitely stated to be the disciple's prayer; and on the lips of a disciple this prayer has its full meaning.[25]

25. Barclay, "Vol. 1," *The Gospel of Matthew*, p. 199.

In this Prayer we see the outline of how to address God and what things we are to pray about. We will take a closer look at this model and see how it will affect, and possibly change, how we approach God. The prayer begins with, "After this manner therefore pray ye: Our Father which art in heaven, hollowed be thy name." (Matthew 6:9 KJV) In all the countries I have visited with different religions, such as Hinduism, Islam and Buddhism, one thing I have found is that none of them have a god they address as father. Their gods may bless sometimes and do evil to them at other times. One god may produce a fruitful harvest and another god may cause an earthquake that kills thousands of people. How wonderful to have a God we can call Father who loves us with an everlasting love! This is the Father that gave His only begotten Son for us. When Jesus was speaking to Nicodemus He said, "For God so loved the world that he gave his only begotten son, that whosoever believeth in him should not perish, but have everlasting life." (John 3:16 KJV) With a great love the Father gave his Son for us, not holding back even that which was most precious to him. When we accept the gift of God in Jesus Christ, we will not be lost or see the destructive fires of Hell.

For the Jewish people God's name is hallowed or holy. Some will not even say his name. When I was in Israel I visited the "Wailing Wall." There Jews and people from all over the world gather to pray. One thing I noticed was that the Orthodox Jews kept bowing periodically as they stood before the Wall praying. Our Senior Pastor, Wallace Heflin, who headed up the Tour, told us every time they say the name of God, they bow in reverence. How wonderful to see such respect for God in a day and time when hearing people take God's name in vain can be frequent in some places! Jesus wants us to pray recognizing that God's name is holy, and it is a privilege to pray to Him.

The next part of the prayer is, "Thy kingdom come; thy will be done in earth, as it is in heaven." (Matthew 6:10 KJV) This word *kingdom* is the Greek word *basileia* which means *royalty, rule or a realm.*[26] The Kingdom is made up of a group of people (the Saints) who belong to the King--Jesus. The Apostle Peter said, "But ye are a chosen generation, a royal priesthood, an holy nation, a peculiar people; that ye should shew forth the praises of

---

26. Strong, *Strong's Exhaustive Concordance of The Bible*, p. 18, # 932.

him who hath called you out of darkness into his marvelous light. (1 Peter 2:9 KJV) The people of God, who represent God, make up that Kingdom. It is composed of the Saints of all the ages. As ambassadors of the Kingdom, we represent God on the earth where we show forth the light of God to a dark world. God has made His people to be leaders in the earth. Too often we just follow what everyone else is doing and pick up a mentality of "whatever will be, will be." The Lord wants us to speak faith and declare the will of God. In doing so, we will provoke the ungodly to Jesus.

We live in times when most people in the United States of America have gotten used to great excess. Almost every family has at least two cars, lives in a nice house, and their cupboards are full of groceries. Many people I know get nervous if they do not have more than enough. All of us need to remember that God is in control and provides every day, as it says in the next verse, "Give us this day our daily bread." (Matthew 6:11 KJV) This part of the prayer takes care of what is happening right now. Jesus will take care of every situation as it arrives. If your electric bill is not due for two weeks, do not get upset because the money is not in the bank. When the bill is due, the provision will be made. Whenever our finances get low, I just say to my wife, "God is going to do a miracle." Usually within a day or two, we will get an unexpected (in the natural) check in the mail, which was usually dated and sent before we recognized the need. Before "today" came, God was already making provision! Praise His name! In Exodus 16:1-21 we find the story of God providing manna for the children of Israel. They were told to gather just enough for their daily provision. If they gathered more, it would spoil. What a wonderful lesson! What we have today is enough for today.

The next part of the prayer is about forgiveness. "And forgive us our debts, as we forgive our debtors." (Matthew 6:12 KJV) The definition of debt is sin, trespass, a state of owing, or something owed.[27] Every one of us has a debt of sin from our past. We all have things we have done wrong that we would like to forget. This is the part of the Lord's Prayer that takes care of our past. I have met Christians who have been raised in a Christian home and have gone to church since childhood. Some feel they have always loved and served Jesus and have never sinned.

---

27. *Webster's New Collegiate Dictionary*, ed. Henry Bosley Woolf (Springfield, MA: G & C Merriam Company, 1981), 289.

However, the Bible says, “For all have sinned, and come short of the glory of God.” (Romans 3:23 KJV) Not one of us was born perfect, that is why we need a Savior.

A very important fact to note about this prayer is the request that God forgive us as we forgive others. Many times we desire quick forgiveness from family, friends, and God, but when it comes to forgiving others, we do not want to let go of things so easily. In my life I have heard comments like, “It is just too much for me to forgive.” Or “I can forgive, but I cannot forget.” No matter how great the sin, there should be forgiveness. God has forgiven all of our sins, even the vilest ones that no one knows about.

Years ago I was a part of a group of brothers from Calvary Pentecostal Tabernacle who went to minister at a men’s prison every Sunday night. We saw such wonderful salvations and great miracles in those meetings. At one point a new brother wanted to be a part of the group to go each week. He had to go through a background check, be fingerprinted, and go on a tour of the prison in order to be familiar with the facility and be informed of what was acceptable behavior there. After the coordinator had shown us around, he said to me, "Do you know the difference between the inmates here and yourself?" I was waiting to hear a response from him like, "You are preachers and live holy lives." Or, "You do not have a prison record." But this is what he said. "You did not get caught." I was very surprised by that, but realized it was the truth. Most of us have done things that were wrong and could have even ended up in jail, but we just were not arrested or no one ever discovered it.

Even after the outline prayer is over, Jesus goes on to emphasize the prerequisite of forgiveness. "For if ye forgive men their trespasses, your heavenly Father will also forgive you: But if ye forgive not men their trespasses, neither will your Father forgive your trespasses." (Matthew 6:14-15 KJV) In these two verses we see what a great power lies in forgiveness. If we pardon others for their transgressions against us, then God will pardon us. The way to experience the full effects of forgiveness is to forgive others of their transgressions toward us. Actually, according to this Scripture, the only way to get forgiveness is to give forgiveness.

Jesus then goes on to say that if we do not pardon others, we will not receive pardon. A good number of Christians harbor unforgiveness which means they will not receive forgiveness from the Lord. Indeed, unforgiveness is sin. Furthermore, Scripture says, "If I regard iniquity in my heart, the Lord will not hear me." (Psalms 66:18 KJV) Many times we get concerned that the Lord is not replying to our prayers. One major cause of unanswered prayer is unforgiveness in our lives. We must examine our hearts regularly, and determine if we are harboring a grudge, then choose to forgive. Ask for God's grace to forgive. We must let go of every hurt, rejection, and wrong done to us—release the grievances, as well as those who perpetrated them, to God. This clears the channel between us and God so that our prayers are heard, and we can experience the victory that comes from walking with Him in total forgiveness.

As we come to the last verse of the Lord's Prayer, let us remember that last does not mean least. The Prayer is not complete without this verse. In previous verses we have seen what was important to take care of the past and present. Here we see what is essential to handle the future in order to be ready to go forth in triumph. "And lead us not into temptation, but deliver us from evil: For thine is the kingdom, and the power, and the glory forever. Amen." (Matthew 6:13 KJV) I like the way the Amplified version of the Bible reads: "And lead (bring) us not into temptation, but deliver us from the evil one. For Yours is the Kingdom and the power, and the glory forever. Amen." (Matthew 6:13 AMP) When we pray this, we are asking God not to even let us get near temptation. There are so many temptations around us everyday—in the workplace, in school, and especially on television and the internet. We can carelessly have an attitude that just a little bit of compromise will not hurt us. However, just one exposure to sin will bring corruption into our lives. Our desire should be to that we not even be touched by temptation and that we be delivered from every attack of the devil. Remember, fleeing from temptation is a very courageous act!

As we end this Prayer, we need to remember everything belongs to God. It is His kingdom, His power, and His glory. When we live in submission to Him, there are many gifts we are privileged to hold in our possession. However, if we begin to think that they are ours and abuse them, the same God that imparted them will be the One who takes them from us.

The last word of this Prayer is Amen. In the Hebrew it means *sure, so be it, truth.*[28] Putting an amen at the end of our prayers means we are saying what we have prayed for is sure, truthful and the way God wants it to be. When we operate according to God's plan of prayer, we will stand on a firm foundation and never be disappointed.

---

28. James Strong, "Hebrew and Chaldee Dictionary," in *Strongs's Exhaustive Concordance of The Bible* (McLean, VA: MacDonald Publishing Company, n.d.), p. 14, # 543.

Chapter 4

The Rock of Faith

In the last chapter we covered much about prayer. That intimate relationship with God is precious, and it will produce a walk of faith. This is a walk filled with miracles that the Lord will do in our lives. However, He does not just want us to be recipients, but participants. In Matthew Chapter fourteen we see the feeding of the five thousand. What a great miracle when Jesus took two fish and some bread and fed the multitude! It only took a little for Jesus to do a lot! On many of my mission trips overseas, I left with a little bit of money to be gone for several months. Looking back I wonder how I did it. It was truly a walk of faith, and that faith is built on a rock.

When we walk in faith, our motives are put to the test. After recording the miracle of the feeding of the five thousand, John in his Gospel writes, “Then those men, when they had seen the miracle that that Jesus did, said, ‘This is of a truth that prophet that should come into the world.’ When Jesus therefore perceived that they would come and take him by force, to make him a king, he departed again into a mountain alone." (John 6:14-15 KJV) These men thought Jesus was the answer to all of their problems. They had watched him feed thousands, surely he could meet every other need as well. It is easy to be flattered when many are patting you on the back, but I have learned to be suspicious when people come around full of compliments. Many times they have selfish motives. These men probably thought Jesus was their ticket to stardom, so to speak. We know Jesus' disciples spent much time wondering which of them would have the greatest position in His kingdom. He knew they would readily agree with making Him king. So this is what Jesus did. "And straightway Jesus constrained his disciples to get into a ship, and to go before him unto the other side, while he sent the multitude away." (Matthew 14:22 KJV) He did not trust his disciples to send the crowd away, he knew for their sakes he needed to do it himself. He had the vision of the cross and what would come in the future and nothing could be allowed to prevent that.

When Jesus compelled His disciples to get into the boat, it was as though He did it by force. The word for *constrained* in the

Greek is *anagkazo* which means *to necessitate.*[29] It was necessary to protect them from their own need for unrealistic power and position. Many ministers need to ask the Lord for the same protection today. Indeed I believe God allows some drastic changes to happen in our lives in order for us to escape some spiritually deadly pit falls. We may feel God surely has a big position or well-paying job for us, but it would only corrupt us and take us out of the center of His will. By putting them in the boat, it would seem Jesus also put them right in the path of a storm. Though most would not think this to be the correct move, often the storms of life are just stepping stones to the greatest miracles we have ever seen.

Some people never like to be alone. They must always have someone with them or at least have the noise of a radio or television playing in their room. However, the best way to hear from the Lord and not allow the message to be contaminated is to get alone with Him. Jesus seemed to know this. "And when he had sent the multitudes away, he went up into a mountain apart to

---

29. Ibid, p.18, # 932.

pray: And when the evening was come he was there alone." (Matthew 14:23 KJV) Jesus needed communion alone with God so He could hear His voice and walk in miracles. He would not be ready to walk on water if He did not have that relationship with the Father.

In the next verse the scene changes from the mountain where Jesus is praying to the disciples in the boat. They are now in the middle of a terrible storm. I can even imagine them thinking, 'Jesus got us into this.' However, it was not for their hurt or destruction, but for their good. It was getting them ready to see Jesus in an entirely new way. It is during the storms of life that true faith is developed. It is then that we learn to look to Jesus and follow His example of walking in miracles. When all seemed lost, Jesus came to them. From where He had been praying on the mountain, he had been able to see His disciples in the middle of the storm. This was one of the sudden storms that the lake was famous for.[30] It is so similar to the sudden storms that happen in our lives. At one moment everything seems just fine—we are having a good

---

30. Barclay, "Vol. 2," *The Gospel of Matthew*, 104.

time of fellowship with family and friends with not a problem in sight. Then, out of nowhere, catastrophe strikes. “And in the fourth watch of the night Jesus went unto them walking on the sea.” (Matthew 14:25 KJV) In ancient times the night was divided into four watches: 6 p.m. to 9 p.m., 9 p.m. to 12 Midnight, 12 Midnight to 3 a.m., and 3 a.m. to 6 a.m.[31] So the time that Jesus came to His disciples was between 3 a.m. and 6 a.m. This is the darkest part of the night. We have all had those dark experiences when it seemed as if we would not see the light of day ever again. All hope was gone. Now, added to the darkness, was a terrible storm. Things were at the very worst they could possibly be, but hope is on the way.

Jesus comes to them in the time of crisis when it seemed He was nowhere around. He came in a miraculous way; not by natural means. He did not row out to them in another boat or, as some theologians have tried to imply, walk out on some form of land bridge. The word *walking* in Verse 25 is the Greek word *peripateo* which means *to tread all around or to walk at large.*[32]

---

31. Ibid, p. 105.

Jesus was walking all over the water, not just in a certain area. The Lord knows how to walk all over every troubled storm. He has that authority and when He walks on water, it will become like a rock and have a foundation that can be stood upon by faith.

When the disciples saw Jesus they were afraid. In the midst of any crisis there can be a great battle with fear. The uncertainty of life's situations are many, and being in a storm such as the disciples were in, I am sure, thoughts of impending death were foremost in their minds. As I have traveled to different nations, I have learned that in a number of cultures there is the belief that if you are close to death, you will begin to get visits from people in the next world. Perhaps this was what the disciples assumed was happening to them. They were very troubled by the presence of this "ghost." Had he come for them? Was death imminent? Would this be their last time out on the Sea of Galilee? Many of these disciples were fishermen. Probably all of them had lost friends and family members in storms on this same lake. Now I am sure they were thinking, "Is this my time?"

---

32. Strong, *Strong's Exhaustive Concordance of The Bible*, p. 1104, # 4043.

Finally, the fear was so great, they screamed out loud. It could not be kept bottled up any longer. Most men do not like to be seen as being afraid of anything and especially prefer that other men do not observe them demonstrating fear or cowardly behavior. However, in an extreme situation like this, all inhibition goes out the window, so to speak. When Jesus heard them cry out, He immediately spoke to them. They were His disciples and He was ready to reassure them and bring peace to their hearts. As we follow Him, He will bring that same comfort to us. All we have to do is cry out to Him. He said, "...Be of good cheer; it is I: be not afraid." (Matthew 14:27 KJV) I really like how the Amplified Version of the Bible puts it. "But instantly, He spoke to them, saying Take courage! I AM! Stop being afraid." (Matthew 14:27 AMP) His instructions were that God was present, and they needed to make a conscious effort to not be afraid anymore. We can let fear come in and overwhelm us, or we can reject it and let the strength of God be in our hearts.

After Peter heard Jesus speak he said, "...Lord, if it be thou, bid me come unto thee on the water." (Matthew 14:28 KJV) I have heard a number of ministers teach that Peter was very impetuous and always spoke before he thought. Indeed, that may have been his nature to an extent, but I believe in this case it was an enormous act of faith. Acting in response to the Lord's voice always requires faith, but doing the supernatural in response to the Word of God requires great faith. Peter knew that what he saw Jesus doing was miraculous, and he wanted to do it as well. That should also be our desire. We should not just be content to hear about Jesus' miracles. Jesus even told His disciples, "I assure you, most solemnly I tell you, if anyone steadfastly believes in Me, he will himself be able to do the things that I do; and he will do even great things than these, because I go to the Father." (John 14:12 AMP) Jesus' own promise is that we will do the miracles He did, and we will even see more done. Jesus' ministry was only three and a half years long, so most of us will have more time in ministry than He did to see the miraculous take place.

Then Jesus said to Peter, "Come, and when Peter was come down out of the ship, he walked on the water to go to Jesus." (Matthew 14:29 KJV) The word *come* here is from the Greek word *eltho* which means *to come or go* and carries the implication of *to accompany, appear, bring, enter, fall out, or grow.*[33] Jesus was literally saying to Peter, "Come, and accompany Me on the water." He wanted Peter to do the same miracle and to enter into that same miracle-working power. Jesus wants us to step out of the boat and put our faith into action, so we can experience His miracle-working power. Taking steps of faith like this will cause us to be stretched spiritually, and this will cause our faith level to rise.

As we grow in faith we learn that it is not feelings that are the greatest evidence of our faith. Our feelings can discourage and even deceive us. On my second missionary journey to Kenya in 1988, I was asked to go speak in a small, remote village called Ogwedy. It was not even near any small town, much less a large city. It took me a considerable amount of time to get there, the last stretch on foot. I arrived just before lunch time and was greeted with a very warm welcome. While the ladies of the church prepared lunch, they gave me a cold soda to drink. As I drank it and fellowshipped with the pastor and church leaders, I began to feel extremely sick. Even though the sun was shining, in my world

---

33. Ibid, p. 204, # 2064.

it was growing very dark. I had contracted malaria and, since I had not experienced it before, was not sure what was happening to me.

When lunch arrived, I was too sick to eat and just continued to sip on my soda. I kept hoping I would start feeling better, and I would have been relieved if someone else could have taken the service that day. However, I was the visiting American missionary and was expected to preach. As I stood to minister, I could hardly hold myself up. I put my hand on a table and used it for support as I brought the Word of the Lord. When I finished the message and gave the altar call for needs, I would have preferred that no one come up for prayer. If anyone needed prayer it was me, but I was the one expected to petition God for everyone else. Almost to my terror, the first person to come up for prayer was a woman who was about thirty-five years old. She had broken her leg just above the knee a few years earlier, but had not gone to the hospital for medical attention. Thus, her leg had healed crooked. It was twisted at about a ninety degree angle. It looked absolutely horrible, and as I laid my hands on her head to pray, I thought, "O Lord, only You can do this." As I prayed, I spoke the Word of God and quoted healing Scripture: "But he was wounded for our transgression, he was bruised for our iniquities: the chastisement of our peace was upon him; and with his stripes we are healed." (Isaiah 53:5 KJV) "I am the Lord that healeth thee." (Exodus 15:26 KJV) So even though I did not feel good physically or even feel full of faith spiritually, I knew who Jesus was and knew how to pray the prayer of faith. As I finished praying, I lifted my hands from her head. I was in for an astonishing sight. The leg that had been broken and twisted was now as straight as the other leg. Praise the Lord! Everyone there was amazed as they watched her walk perfectly and without assistance. What a true miracle from God! I had gotten out of the boat, so to speak, and the Lord had not disappointed me.

When we trust in Jesus and all He has told us, He will always stand behind His Word. When Peter got out of the boat, he was walking on the water just like Jesus was walking on the water. It was the same miraculous power, and he could do it because he trusted in the voice of the Master. As long as he walked toward Jesus and kept his eyes focused on the Lord, there was no problem at all doing the miraculous. The same can be said of us; as long as we walk toward Him and keep our eyes on Him, we will live right, act right, and walk in miracles. It is only when we remove our vision from the Lord that issues will get out of hand in our lives. "But when he saw the wind boisterous, he was afraid; and beginning to sink, he cried, saying, Lord save me." (Matthew 14:30 KJV) The moment he took his eyes off of Jesus, he became aware again of the intensity of the storm. He could feel the force of the wind and see the waves as they rose up high enough to knock down even a strong man. Fear filled his heart, and faith ran away in great haste. One moment he was a water walking disciple, the next he was sinking. It only takes a moment to lose what we have gained in Christ. The storms of life can be many and will come from every direction. But no matter what issues we have to face, we must keep our attention on Jesus. We see that as Simon Peter began to sink, he called to Jesus. I believe that as soon as he began to sink, he cried to Jesus. He did not wait until he was about to go under and die from drowning to call out to the Lord. He called as soon as he began to go under. What a tremendous lesson can be learned from Peter: As soon as we slip, we should call out immediately and loudly. The God we serve will always answer us. He did not call to his fellow disciples back in the boat or call in the name of a heathen god who could not hear him, but he called on the name of the Lord. He knew where his help would come from.

Let us be those who know where our help comes from. "I will call upon the Lord, who is worthy to be praised: so shall I be saved from mine enemies." (Psalm 18:3 KJV) Often when trouble strikes we call upon everyone else. We talk to family on the phone, share with our buddies at the gym, or converse with our neighbors across the fence. Then, only as a last resort, we tell Jesus. Sometimes we might think sharing with others is the easy way, but really it is the most difficult. In the end, when we finally go to Jesus, we find He has all the answers and was the One we should have approached first.

"And immediately Jesus stretched forth his hand, and caught him and said unto him, O thou of little faith, wherefore didst thou doubt?" (Matthew 14:31 KJV) Promptly the Lord came to his aide. He grabbed ahold of Peter with a firm grip that just would not let go. Then He spoke to Peter and corrects him for having small or limited faith. Some may think Jesus was being to harsh, but I personally do not think so. When someone has grown to the point or large faith that walks on water, it is a sad day when they retreat and have little faith. A dear and long-time friend of mine, Apostle Charles Davidson from Clarksville, Virginia, hosts a Men's Advance each November, which the brothers from our Church have attended for the past nine years. He said, regarding the reason they call it an Advance, "I refuse to call this a retreat because we are not retreating here. We are advancing." Praise God! It is never a time to go back in faith, but we must move forward.

"And when they were come into the ship, the wind ceased." (Matthew 14:32 KJV) Jesus and Peter walked back to the boat together. We often do not take time to consider that Peter walked the same distance back to the boat the he had walked away from it. He did it by faith, and he did it with Jesus. The Lord wanted him to accompany Him on the water, and Peter did just that. When they stepped into the boat the wind stopped. The vessel and all those in it had been tormented in the storm, but when Jesus got into the vessel the storm was over. It is the same in our lives. Jesus will calm our storm and bring peace in the middle of confusion. Once the other disciples saw that Jesus had walked on the water, saw Peter walk on the water through faith in Jesus, and saw the storm calmed by His presence, they recognized His majesty and power as the Son of God. "Then they that were in the ship came and worshipped him, saying, Of a truth thou art the Son of God." (Matthew 14:33 KJV) The God of miracles was among them, and they had seen Him with their own eyes walking on the troubled Sea. When we have seen the acts of the Lord first hand, we have what seasoned saints call "an experience."

When I first moved to Calvary Pentecostal Tabernacle in Ashland, Virginia to be trained in ministry back in 1981, I began hearing great stories of miracles, healings, and mass salvation campaigns abroad. I felt very insecure about going abroad since I was just a country boy from North Carolina who did not even leave the State until I was eighteen years old. My experiences were very limited, and all this talk of great exploits overwhelmed me. I thought to myself, "How will I ever get there? Who would pay for my air ticket? No one knows me." But I was to learn that the great God of the universe knew who I was, where I was, and how to get me to where He wanted me, too! During an evening service in which Rev. Jane Lowder was ministering, she began to pray for people at the altar. Many were getting prophetic words from the

Lord through her, and as she got closer to me, I hoped I would receive one as well. After several weeks of living away from home, I was very homesick. I missed my family, my car, and my good-paying job at Cutter Laboratories. Even though I knew I had heard God's voice in my move to Ashland, I was ready for further instruction. When Sister Jane reached me, she began to speak over me. God said, "I am going to put your feet on many different soils." I knew He was saying that I would go to the nations and I believed it. I did not know where or when, and with no experience in preaching or teaching, what I would even say when I did go.

About a week later, I was asked to speak at the Youth Service one evening. I was literally scared to death. I was not sure of a topic and certainly had no missionary stories to tell as others did. I went to my dorm to pray and seek the Lord about what I could share. As I leafed through my Bible, I turned to a portion of Scripture in the book of Luke. It said, "Remember Lot's wife. Whosoever shall seek to save his life shall lose it; and whosoever shall lose his life shall preserve it." (Luke 17:32-33 KJV) Those verses really spoke to my heart. I had begun my walk of faith and stepped out of the boat, now God was telling me not to look back.

I preached that evening from that passage. The message was only five minutes long with me repeating a number of statements over and over. I hoped someone in the audience got blessed, but I was keenly aware that the message was primarily for me. A few days later the Lord spoke to me that I would go to Haiti. I knew that would be my first mission trip, but I was not sure what would come after that. I guess I thought Jesus would not tell me too much or require too much of me at one time. I was in for a lot of surprises!

A couple of weeks later, I was praying face down in church, when the Lord spoke to me that I would go to Kenya, South Africa, and China. I was excited, but somewhat amazed. I had not even gone to Haiti yet, and God was already speaking to me about going to other nations as well. It was like He wanted me to keep hearing Him and be prepared always to go in His direction. The next year was filled with training by way of church meetings, monthly seminars, and finally my first ten and ½ weeks of camp meeting.

During Summer Camp Meeting 1982, many people on staff were getting blessed with finances for their mission trips abroad.

However, I received no money at all. I wondered, “Is it working for others, but not for me?” When Camp Meeting was over, I went home to visit my family. There was a surprise waiting for me. My father had filed my income taxes for 1981 when I had worked for Cutter Laboratories and, to my amazement, I received a refund big enough to purchase my air ticket to Haiti and have plenty left over for spending money! I had never gotten a tax refund before while working at Cutter, so I never expected this blessing.

In December 1982 I went to Haiti with a group led by my uncle, Rev. Lloyd Ashby of Sanford, North Carolina. We ministered up in the mountains and helped build pews for a church down in the capitol city of Port-au-Prince. I had never seen such poverty, but I did not feel any discouragement. I had gone for God, and it was just the beginning of following Him.

After returning from Haiti there was more training, and soon it was time for Summer Camp Meeting again. It was a wonderful summer in God as we worshipped and received from the Lord. As a part of the Camp staff, I also worked very hard without a salary, but I knew the Lord was my Employer and He would pay right well. During a particular evening service the Lord blessed greatly and $50,000 was raised for missionary travel. Everyone on staff was excited and began to plan their itineraries overseas. Then they visited Brother Heflin's (the director of the Camp at that time) office to talk to him about the places they believed they were being called and get his approval. I was busy working and was confident that there was plenty of time to plan my trip. God had shown me this would be the year for Kenya and South Africa. I had already talked with Sister Ruth Carneal, a mother in the faith, about traveling with her group that was going to those two countries as well as several other African nations. As Camp Meeting ended, people began flying off in every direction, and I thought, "It is now time to go talk to Brother Heflin and schedule mine as well." I was shocked to find that all the money had been used for other staff members' trips, and there was nothing left.

For the next couple of months I went through a time of great questioning. I knew I had heard God about where to go, but there was no money to go there. "What went wrong?" I thought. As I prayed during that time, I came to realize God was in control of everything, and that it was His plan and not mine. At Thanksgiving time, Rev. George Slaughter announced he would be traveling to Kenya in January. Brother Slaughter was a member of the Board of Trustees for Calvary Pentecostal Tabernacle and a seasoned missionary from Little Plymouth, Virginia. I became excited, hoping that maybe I could go with him. I was delighted when he agreed to take me. I talked with Brother Heflin about this and after praying, God provided a ticket to Kenya and South Africa for me.

Brother Slaughter and I arrived in Kisumu, Kenya in January of 1984. We spent our first night at the YMCA. The family that had hosted Brother Slaughter on a previous trip did not have a telephone and lived just outside the city of Kisumu. He was hoping to be able to locate them the next day. In the morning we checked out of the YMCA and had brunch at a local restaurant. Afterwards we were walking along the street when a young Kenyan woman ran out from a business along the street and greeted Brother Slaughter. Her name was Phanice Gweya, and she was the daughter of the pastor he had worked though previously. By nightfall we were at the Gweya's house in a little village about five miles outside of Kisumu. Pastor Gweya opened many doors for us, and for the next two months we were preaching two or three times a day mostly in village churches. Brother Slaughter required me to preach at least once a day. He told me that before we left America, Brother Heflin had told him to "push me out of the boat." Indeed, he did! In the beginning when I would preach, Brother Slaughter would tell me I did not go long enough. I worked hard to come up with new, relevant sermons and began to grow in my delivery.

We preached in many different churches, but the one place we saw the greatest results was at the church where Brother Gweya was the pastor. People were saved, healed, and filled with the Holy Spirit in every service. One night the village drunk came to the service. He was about thirty years old, drunk, and very dirty. He probably had not bathed in six months. During the praise and worship, he would make strange sounds, trying to disturb us. Each time we would quiet him down and continue praising the Lord. Finally, on the fourth night, instead of trying to stop him from making a disturbance, we asked him if he would like to get saved. He said, "Yes. I would like to get saved." We led him in the sinner's prayer and finished the service. The next night, he came to church sober and cleaned up. He came to every service after that, and by the time I left Kenya six weeks later, he was serving as one of my interpreters! Today he is a pastor in Kenya. Praise the Lord!

After the first month in Kenya, Brother Slaughter returned to the USA. I was on my own. I still preached somewhere every day. It was a new step knowing I had no one else on which to rely, but Jesus. Everything I learned from Brother Slaughter had to be implemented. It was a time of growth and seeing that God could use me as well.

One day Pastor Gweya came to me and said, "You will be preaching this Sunday in the church at Shinglalu." This news was very exciting for me because Brother Slaughter had preached there when we had first arrived in the country about five weeks earlier. It was a very big church that had about two thousand people in the Sunday morning service. As a young twenty-four year old minister, I was bursting with pride that I had been asked to speak to such a large congregation. When the weekend finally arrived, I was ready with the right message that would bless and leave a lasting impression with the folks of the church at Shinglalu.

When we arrived at the Church, I was thinking of how full the church was last time we were there. It would be great to see an enormous crowd like that again. As my interpreter and I walked through the front doors of the sanctuary, I was met with total shock. There were only about four people up at the front of the Church talking. My first thought was, "They heard a young preacher was coming and decided not to show up."

When we reached the front, the pastor told us a little boy of two years old, the son of a lady who was a member of the congregation, had died and the funeral was to be held that morning at their home. So we began to walk to the distant home where the funeral was to be held. On the way, my interpreter told me that it was Kenyan custom to have the funeral at the home of the deceased and the body would be buried in their own yard. As we walked on a little further, the pastor said, "You will be preaching the funeral." I was shocked. I had never preached a funeral before, not even in America. I was not sure I was ready for the task, and there was no time to prepare.

When we arrived at the family compound, someone was already speaking, and for a moment I thought that another minister was doing the service. We sat down and began listening. My interpreter told me that the man speaking was a government official. In Kenya the government sends a representative to every wedding and funeral in rural areas in order to make announcements. The man was expressing what the government required of its citizens. Then he said, "If you do all these correctly, the Bible says there will be 144,000 in heaven and you could be one of them if you do all the right things." I knew where he had heard that doctrine. It is taught by a very popular cult. When I got up to preach, I looked out at a massive group of people. Every church and family in the area had come to be represented. I began to speak about heaven and our need for salvation through the shed blood of Jesus Christ. Then I said, "I never knew this little boy on the earth, but one day I will walk on streets of gold with him." As I ended my message, I felt moved to have an altar call for whoever wanted to accept Jesus as their Savior. Over two hundred people came forward to surrender their lives to Christ. Even the government official got saved! Praise the Lord! If we had had the Sunday service as planned in the Church, maybe fifteen or more would have been saved, but the Lord knew where the souls were.

He also knew how to push me out of the boat to do my first funeral.

After the service was over, we returned to the Church where the pastor gave us some gifts for coming to visit them. Then we headed to the local bus stop to get a matatu for the journey home. It was getting late in the evening, and we were about thirty miles from our home base. Since most forms of public transportation come to a halt at around six p.m., we were rushing to secure a ride. As we were about to get on a matatu, I saw a man sitting beside the road. The Lord said to me, "Go and tell him about Me." I told my interpreter what God had spoken to me, and we went to speak to the gentleman. There beside the road, with busy traffic moving all around us, he gave his life to Jesus. We gave him the names of several good churches in the area, and encouraged him to attend. I learned that day that God is interested in each individual soul. The man beside the road was just as important as the two hundred that were saved at the funeral. Jesus is still looking to save the lost.

Once we finished witnessing to him, we went into a small shop and bought cold sodas. Coming out of the shop, we started across the road to try to catch another ride home, when my interpreter's cousin, who lived in the area, drove by in his own personal car. He stopped and gave us a ride all the way home. I realized that because we were faithful to witness to that one man, the Lord was faithful to get us a quick ride home.

My time in Kenya was about to be over. I had booked my ticket to leave on the 14th of March because that was the date God had spoken to me to go to South Africa. My first week in Kenya, I had written one of the contacts in South Africa given to me by a missionary friend in Ashland. Their names were Freddy and Anna Janssen. I told them when I would arrive. But, the day came to leave and I had not received any reply from them. When I got on the plane to fly to South Africa, I said to God, "I do not know where I will be tonight, but I know I will be with You."

When I landed in Johannesburg, I tried to call Freddy and Anna. There was no answer. So I called the number of another person I had been given back in Ashland. They said they would come and pick me up. After we had lunch, they drove me to Freddy and Anna's house. As we approached the house, Anna was driving into their driveway, and we followed her in the yard. She welcomed me to stay with them, and I was very glad to have somewhere to stay that night. After I was settled, and we were having tea, she said, "Sister Ruth has been staying here, and she is now over at my mother-in-law's house." I immediately thought she was speaking of Sister Ruth Heflin, the sister of my senior pastor, Rev. Wallace Heflin, Jr., and the Pastor of Mount Zion Fellowship in Jerusalem, Israel. She was always traveling to and fro among the nations, so I immediately assumed it was she they were speaking of. Then Anna said, "It is Ruth Carneal." How faithful is our God! The same person I had originally planned to travel with in Africa was the one I was with before nightfall. I had stepped out by faith, and God was the One who was making all the arrangements.

For the next two weeks Sister Carneal and I ministered in meetings almost every day. In these meetings the prophetic gift was flowing tremendously. Sister Carneal would open up and give words from the Lord individually to fifty people or more in each service. One night after she had preached the Word, she began to minister prophetically over individuals, but after the first person, she pulled me over to minister over the second. When I was finished, I just knew she would minister over the third person, but she pushed me out of the boat and had me minister over the rest of the people in the meeting. I had given a few prophetic words during my brief time in ministry, but I had never stepped out to prophecy over an entire group. My faith was stretched and enlarged again. Indeed, I had found water to stand on!

For weeks before I reached South Africa, Sister Carneal had been trying to leave the country to go to Sierra Leone, West Africa. Each time she went to the Embassy of Sierra Leone to get a visa, she was denied. Because there would be a stopover in the Ivory Coast, she also needed a visa for the Ivory Coast. They had also refused to give her a visa. After we had ministered together for about a week in South Africa, she decided to try again for the visas. This time both embassies immediately gave her visas and me as well. We realized God had kept her there until I arrived so we could travel on together. That evening God spoke to someone to pay for my air ticket to be changed to include Ivory Coast and Sierra Leone. It was all God's plan and God's timing!

When we arrived in Freetown, Sierra Leone, we had the address of Princess James, the sister-in-law of Pastor Ade Jones of

Bethel Temple Assembly of God. We arrived at her house and she took us to church with her that evening. It was a wonderful service where we were able to meet the pastor and his wife. The Church had just started a forty-day revival and on our third night there, they turned all the meetings over to us. We preached for a month, alternating services. What a great time of miracles we had with God working mightily in every service!

About one week before it was time to leave Sierra Leone, having just finished preaching, I turned to Sister Carneal and asked, "How did I do?" She said, "It was very good, but you went too long." I realized that in four months time, I had gone from being an inexperienced minister with little to say, to one who could flow in the gifts and preach a full balanced message and sometimes go too long! I had obeyed God's call and trusted Him to teach me to walk by faith. He had not disappointed me; and He never will!

CONCLUSION

What a wonderful thing it is to know Jesus, especially in the tumultuous day in which we live! At the Calvary Pentecostal Tabernacle in Richmond, Virginia, there was a plaque hanging in front of the pulpit that said, "Jesus Never Fails." Many times that plaque served to remind me Who had called me and His great faithfulness. I received faith and grace to continue standing on the Rock. I have seen Him fulfill His Word again and again in many varied and diverse situations and circumstances, at home and abroad. The Scripture says, "Jesus Christ the same yesterday, and today and forever." (Hebrews 13:8 KJV) Everything else in this life will pass away, but Jesus never changes. So, wise men build their lives upon Jesus—The Rock.

As I continue to serve the Lord , I sing this beautiful hymn with more gusto:

My hope is built on nothing less
Than Jesus' blood and righteousness.
I dare not trust the sweetest frame,
But wholly lean on Jesus' name.

On Christ the solid Rock I stand;

All other ground is sinking sand

All other ground is sinking sand.[34]

---

34. Edward Mote, and William Bradbury, *The Solid Rock*, Public Domain, Christian Copyright Licensing Inc, http://ccli.com.

BIBLIOGRAPHY

Barclay, William. "Vol. 1," In *The Gospel of Matthew*. The Daily Study Bible Series. Revised Edition. Reprint, Philadelphia, PA: The Westminster Press, 1975.

Barclay, William. "Vol. 2." In *The Gospel of Matthew*. The Daily Study Bible Series. Revised Edition. Reprint, Philadelphia, PA: The Westminster Press, 1975..

McClintock, John, and James Strong. "Vol. III - E, F, G." In *Cyclopediea of Biblical, Theological, and Eccesiastical Literature*. New York: Harper & Brothers Publishers, 1883.

Mote, Edward, and William Bradbury. *The Solid Rock*. Public Domain. Christian Copyright Licensing Inc. http://ccli.com.

Strong, James. "Greek Dictionary of The New Testament." In *Strong's Exhaustive Concordance of The Bible*. McLean, VA: MacDonald Publishing Company, n.d

Strong, James. "Hebrew and Chaldee Dictionary." In *Strongs's Exhaustive Concordance of The Bible*. McLean, VA: MacDonald Publishing Company, n.d.

Webster's New Collegiate Dictionary. Edited by Henry Bosley Woolf. Springfield, MA: G & C Merriam Company, 1981.

Weidemann, Viola. *Girded With Strength*. Hagerstown, MD: McDougal Publishing Company, 1997.

About the Author

Dr. Scottie Jackson was born and raised in Four Oaks, NC. He attended a Pentecostal camp meeting and was filled with the Holy Spirit with the evidence of speaking in other tongues at the age of 21. Soon afterward he accepted God's call upon his life and went into full-time ministry.

From 1983 until 1999 he did missionary evangelism in Kenya, South Africa, Nigeria, Sierra Leone, China, Nepal, Philippines, India, Hong Kong, Russia, Dominican Republic, Haiti, Trinidad, Jamaica, and Cuba as well as in the USA.

Since July 1999 he has been pastoring River of Life Pentecostal Church in Colonial Beach, Virginia and also continues to take short-term mission trips a couple times a year, taking along men who desire to be trained in overseas ministry.

In 1989 he married another missionary evangelist, Darlene Brabrand Jackson. They have two children. They are ordained and covered by Pentecostal Faith Assemblies, Inc. In 2005 he became

Bishop of this Fellowship of ministers and ministries. In 2012 he founded Pentecostal Faith Bible Institute over which he presides as Chancellor.

Feel free to contact Dr. Jackson at
P O Box 84
Colonial Beach, VA 22443
pfaibishop@yahoo.com

More Information

Pentecostal Faith Assemblies, Inc.
www.pfai.org.

River of Life Pentecostal Church
www.riveroflifepc.org

40482691R00063

Made in the USA
Middletown, DE
14 February 2017